W9-AWE-150

During her grandmother's memorial service, Emilie, my five-year-old daughter, asked me, "Mom, do they do things like this when babies are born?" I whispered, "Yes, Emilie, there are many ways to say 'hello' to babies."

MBK

Welcoming Babies

Margy Burns Knight

Illustrations by Anne Sibley O'Brien

Tilbury House, Publishers
Gardiner, Maine

Every day, everywhere, babies are born. We have many ways to show them we are glad they came into the world.

We Sing

Afam is a brand new baby. When the women near his house hear his first cry, they begin to sing, "Beautiful one, beautiful one, welcome!" When other women hear the song, they join in. Soon Afam's whole village will know that a new baby has been born.

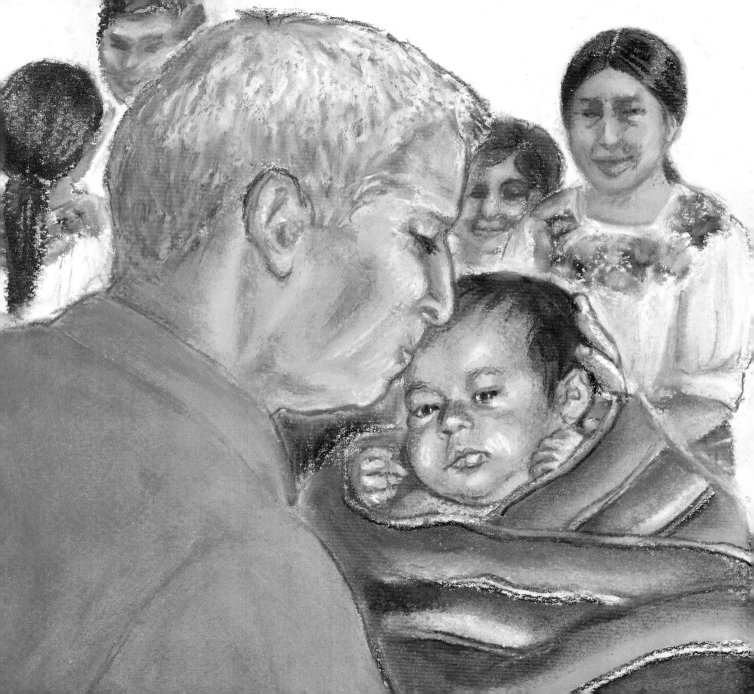

We Kiss

Maria and Tomas are eight days old. Today the door of their home is opened for visitors who greet the twins with kisses. Candles are lit, and a special meal is served to celebrate the birth of the babies.

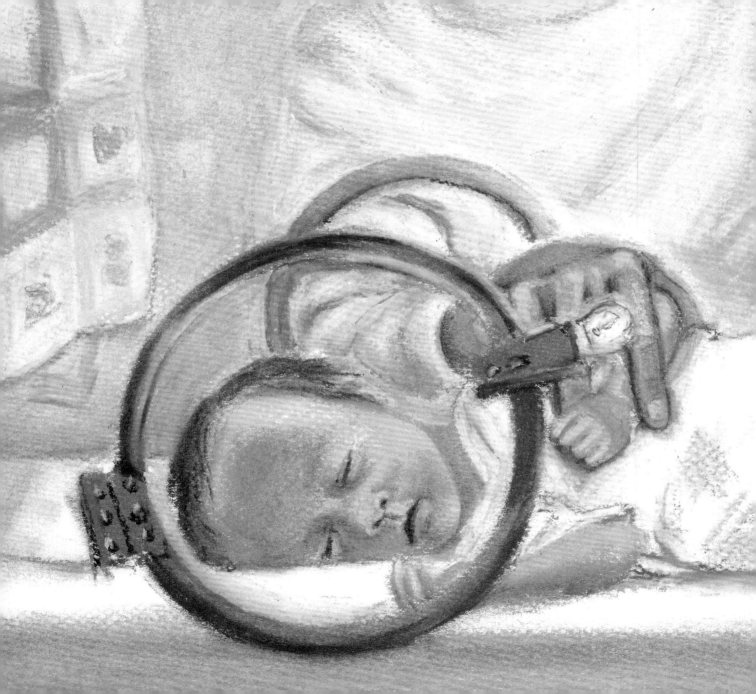

We Touch

Many times every day Luke's parents gently rub him. His cousins sent him a musical doll so he can listen to "My Favorite Things" in his incubator. Nurses and doctors will take good care of Luke until he is ready to go home.

We Bless

A tiny drop of sugar butter is placed on Cyrus's tongue by the midwife so that he will have a sweet life. Soon his grandfather will whisper prayers to Allah into each of Cyrus's ears.

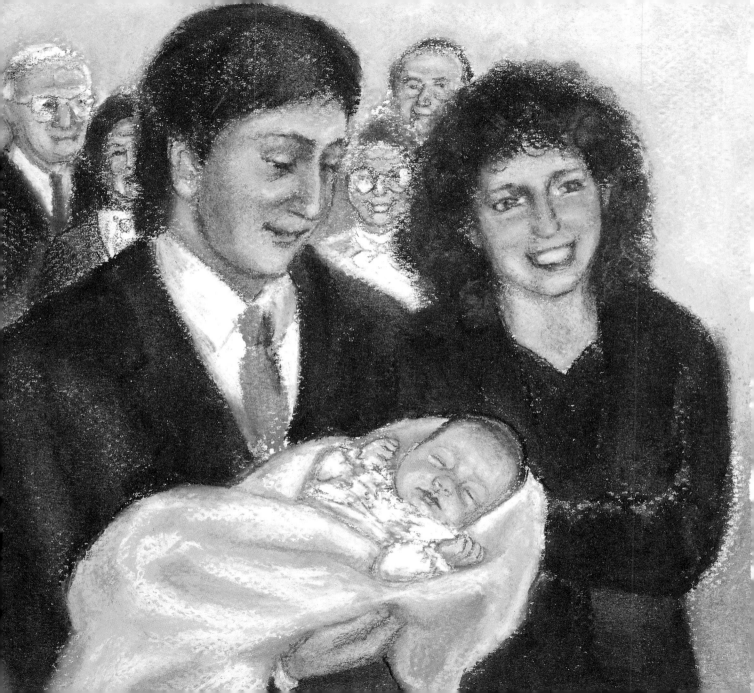

We ame

Jeff and Judi say Hebrew prayers for their infant
daughter Rachel, whom they named for
Jeff's mother. Rabbi Ascher and
the congregation join them in prayer
during Rachel's naming ceremony.

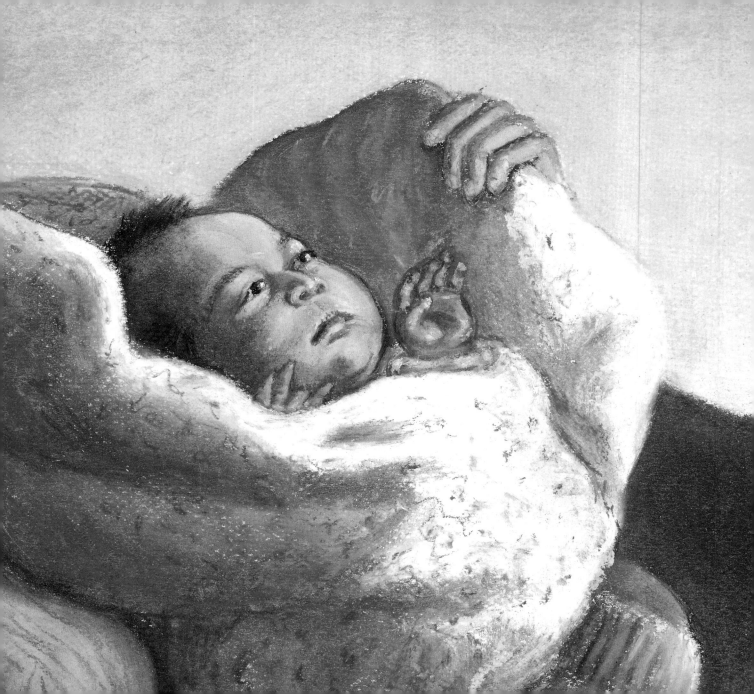

We Greet

Kasa was born twenty days ago, and today is her naming
ceremony. Her grandmother, who chose her name, lifts the
blanket off Kasa's tiny face. She holds her granddaughter
up to greet the first rays of the early morning sun.

We Promise

Reverend Lawson places a drop of water on Alexis's forehead. Her parents promise to teach her about God as she grows. With this baptism, Alexis is welcomed into the Christian church.

We Announce

Lidia and Jason want to tell their friends and family how excited they are about their new sister. The cards they send have two special dates: the day Rosa was born and the day she came into their family by adoption.

Tom, Alice, Jason & Lidia
are happy to announce
the arrival of
Rosa Helena

Born April 16, 1994
São Paulo, Brazil
Came home
August 4, 1994

We Hold

Joseph's friends and relatives sit in a circle during Sunday meeting. Each person holds baby Joseph to greet him. Emilie waits for her turn to say hello to Joseph. She wants to hold him all by herself.

We Celebrate

Carmen loves her new cousin Ricardo. At the christening party given by his godparents, she and the other guests wear *encintados*. These colorful ribbons show the names of Ricardo and his godparents.

We Give gifts

Lia's *yai-yai* shows her granddaughter the presents she placed under her baby pillow the day she was born. In a small piece of cotton she put a sprinkle of sugar, a few grains of rice, and a silver coin so that Lia might have a sweet, sturdy, and rich life. She also gave Lia cotton so that she might live long enough to have white hair.

We Honor

In the springtime following her birth, Baby Anna's family plants her celebration tree. Each year on her September birthday, the leaves of this maple will be bright red.

We Play

Darrell and his father love to play together. Each morning as they get ready for their day, they play the same special games. Darrell always makes his father laugh.

We Treasure

For her first birthday, Ok-hee's family fills the table with gifts and food. Those who treasure her gather to wish Ok-hee a long and happy life.

We share the same wish for all babies everywhere.

Notes

Sing

Afam is an Igbo from Nigeria. In many villages throughout Africa, babies are welcomed with songs.

•A communal cry of joy is sung by women in parts of Morocco to announce to the surrounding neighborhood that a birth has occurred.

•In the United States, Navajos chant a special song at important times in a person's life. "The Blessing Way" is sung as a baby is about to be born. It is thought to ensure health, harmony, and prosperity.

Kiss

Maria and Tomas are Quiché twins who live in Guatemala. For the first eight days of life, Quiché babies stay with their mother, and friends bring food and gifts. On the eighth day the babies are bathed and dressed in new clothes. After the house is cleaned and candles are lit, the doors are opened so that the neighbors and relatives can kiss the babies and have a big feast.

Touch

All babies are touched. Babies who must stay in incubators after they are born may be touched only through holes in the side of the incubator. The parents long for the day they can hold their baby in their arms.

•Massage is a loving touch that many babies all over the world enjoy. In many parts of India, one- to six-month-old babies are massaged regularly by their mothers with coconut or diluted mustard oil. This tradition is often passed down from mother to daughter.

•In the Philippines, a traditionally trained *hilot* massages babies and their mothers.

Bless

Cyrus's parents were born in Afghanistan and are Muslims. In some Afghani families, babies are fed sugar butter for the first six days. The sugar butter also symbolizes cleansing.

•In parts of Pakistan, an elder feeds a new baby *gutki* by putting a fingertip of molasses in the baby's mouth.

•In Senegal, Muslims write prayers from the Koran on a piece of paper. After they soak the paper in water, they tear off a tiny piece and place it on the newborn's tongue. Seven days after birth, the child's name is whispered three times into each ear.

Name

Rachel's ceremony is called *Simchat Bat*, which means "joy of daughter." Her younger brother, Aaron Samuel, had a bris, or *Brit Milah*, which means "covenant of circumcision." Traditionally Jewish children are named after a deceased relative.

•In Tibet, many babies are given a secret name by a *lama*, a high priest in the Buddhist faith. The name is written down and worn in a pouch around the neck for life. Babies are given other names to be used by family and friends.

•In some Vietnamese families, fathers name the sons, and mothers name the daughters.

Greet

Kasa's paternal grandmother gave her a Hopi name. She is a member of the Hopi tribe in the United States. On her twentieth day, Kasa's father watches for the sunrise as a group of women walks with her to greet the sun. Kasa's grandmother says a prayer as she takes the blanket away from her granddaughter's face.

Promise

Many Christian communities use baptism to welcome babies into their faith. The water used during the baptism symbolizes life and cleansing.

•After baptisms in the Philippines, when many babies are christened, godparents run to the door of the church holding their godchild. The first child out of the church may grow up to be a leader.

Announce

Lidia and Jason announced their adopted sister's arrival with a homemade card.

•Some families make phone calls or put a notice in the newspaper to announce the coming of a new baby.

•In ancient Rome, an olive branch for a boy or a strip of woolen fabric for a girl was hung from the front door to announce the baby's arrival.

Hold

Joseph is being welcomed to his Quaker Meeting.

•In Zaire, many Mbuti people welcome babies by standing in a circle and passing the child among them so the baby can be held and greeted by members of the community.

•In some Iranian families, new babies are passed around a circle and each person whispers prayers to Allah into the infant's ears.

Celebrate

Throughout Spanish-speaking Latin America, parties are given by the *campadre* and *camadre*, the godparents, for their godchildren after they are baptized.

•In many Puerto Rican communities, after a feast of roast pig, pigeon peas, and salad, each guest takes home an *encintado*.

Give gifts

Lia's Greek grandma puts cotton, sugar, rice, and coins in a bag for Lia and keeps it in a special place.

•Protective amulets are given to babies in Afghanistan and the Philippines.

•In Cambodia, strings with money attached to them are tied around babies' wrists.

Honor

Anna lives in Maine, and her tree was chosen because of her September birthday. Her brother Nathan's birch tree was planted because Nathan was named after his grandfather, who loved birch trees. Little sister Kimberly's tree is an evergreen because she was born in December.

•In the Jewish ceremony a tree is planted at the birth of a child: a cedar for a boy and a pine for a girl. When a couple marries, their birth trees are cut down and used to build a *huppah*, or wedding pavilion.

•In Switzerland, an apple tree is often planted for the birth of a boy and a nut tree for a girl.

•In the Philippines, a tree is often planted where the umbilical cord was buried.

Play

All over the world people play peek-a-boo with babies. They also play clapping, bouncing, finger, and toe games. Many families have special baby games that they pass down from generation to generation.

Treasure

Ok-hee is Korean. First and sixtieth birthdays are the only two birthdays celebrated in Korea. In all other years, people count themselves a year older on Lunar New Year. The objects on Ok-hee's birthday table are symbols for her future: yarn for a long life, money for wealth, a notebook so she will grow up to be a good student. Rice cakes, candy, and fruit are also on the table.

A special thanks to the following: Jay Hoffman and the University of Maine at Augusta Library, Donna Headrick, Christi and Ricardo Moraga, the Bender family, the Toothaker family, Ifi Amadiume, Reverend Margaret Lawson, Bill Myer, the Claman-Kaledin family, Ali Kahn, Gladys and Burtt Richardson, the Habibzai family, the McIlwain family, Steve Downe, Dianne Webb, Pam Osborn, Nancy McGinnis, Sue Cannon, Teri Grant, Debbie Mihalakies, Steve Notis, Mary Haeri, and Chun Taylor.

Tilbury House, Publishers
132 Water Street
Gardiner, ME 04345

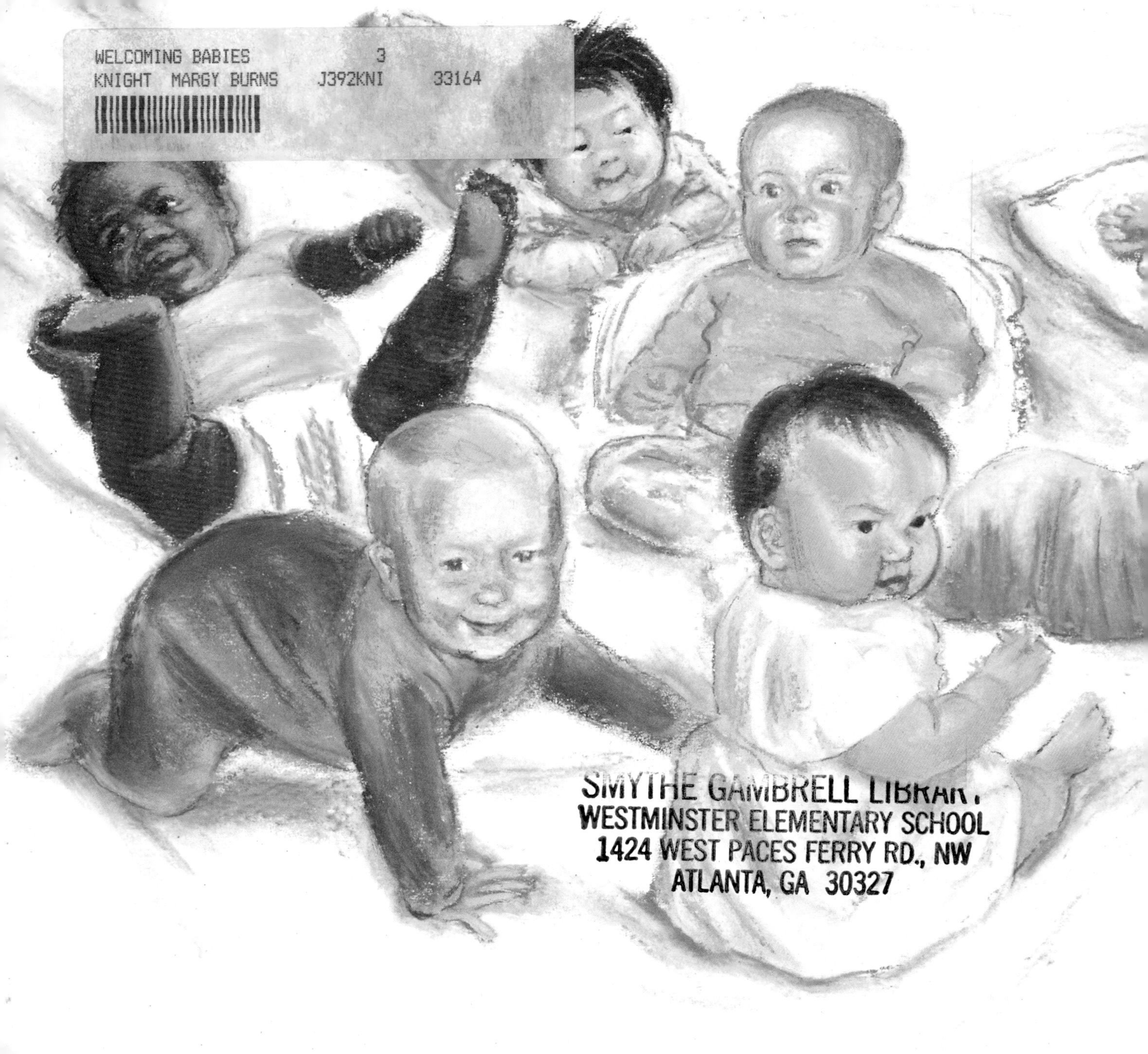